Skipton, 1967

with Pennine, Laycock, Ribble and West Yorkshire buses

Stuart Emmett

Representing the large company stage buses in late 1950s Skipton, are West Yorkshire and Ribble with West Yorkshire DGW8, a Bristol KSW6G on the 67 for Bradford, followed by a Bristol LD on the 76 to Tadcaster, and a Ribble PD3 leaving on the X43 for Manchester. None of these routes were short journeys at respectively, 68, 142 and 153 minutes.

Text © Stuart Emmett, 2020.
First published in the United Kingdom, 2020, reprinted 2023,
by Stenlake Publishing Ltd.,
54-58 Mill Square,
Catrine, Ayrshire,
KA5 6RD

Telephone: 01290 551122
www.stenlake.co.uk

ISBN 9781840338591

Printed by P2D,
1 Newlands Road,
Westoning,
MK45 5LD

The publishers regret that they cannot supply copies of any pictures featured in this book.

Sources

Independent Bus Services in Western, South Eastern and Yorkshire Traffic Areas, Omnibus Society, July 1954.
Independent Bus Services Yorkshire Traffic Area, Omnibus Society, January 1979.
Independent Bus Operators in Yorkshire, Neville Mercer, 2015.
Northern Rose – The history of West Yorkshire, Keith Jenkinson, 1987.
Pennine Motor Services 1925 to 2000, Donald Binns, Trackside Publications, 2000.
Skipton & District Bus Timetable and Railway Guide, October 1961 to June 1962.
The West Yorkshire Road Car Company Limited, Fleet History PB12 Part 2, The PSV Circle, Omnibus Society, West Yorkshire Information Service.
West Yorkshire, Keith Jenkinson, 1977.
West Yorkshire, Timetables for 1961 and 1966 to 1969.

Picture Acknowledgements

Unless stated below, the pictures are from my own collection that is made up of our family pictures and other sources. For the latter, where the original photographer cannot be traced, I offer my apologies to them for the lack of accreditation and would be pleased to be able to correct this in future editions.

Bus Gallery: pages 31, 35.
Bus Photos.co.uk: pages 33, 39, 41, 43, 44.
John Cockshott Archive (The Transport Library): pages 23 (lower), 24, 27.
Mike Jeavons: page6 16, 37.

Omnibus Society: pages 10, 20 (lower).
PM Photography: pages 18, 25, 30, 42.
Travel Lens Photographic: page 9.
J. Walker (from the PSV Circle Collection): page 26.

On Sunday 15th October 1967 we went on a visit to Skipton, Yorkshire. You would expect Sunday to be a quiet day in this small market town that is the "Gateway to the Dales". However, it is a central transport location being at junction of the A65 road (from Leeds and Otley up to the Lake District) and the A59 from York and Harrogate to Liverpool. Skipton, therefore, tends to always be a busy place and this has resulted in some long-distance bus routes. Additionally, it attracts visitors from the small towns and villages in Ribblesdale, Airedale and Wharfedale, including the conurbations of Burnley/Colne and Leeds/Bradford.

In 1967 the town's major employer was Dewhurst's, the manufacturers of Syklo cotton sewing thread who employed 800 people. Fifty years later the largest employer is the Skipton Building Society as Dewhurst's closed many years ago, and their Broughton Road mill, a five storey building, is now apartments. Thomas Spencer was born in Skipton in 1858 and in 1884 co-founded Marks and Spencer in Leeds.

On our journey to Skipton we saw an unusual West Yorkshire bus from Keighley Depot, SRG23, a 1966 Bristol RELL6G with ECW B50D body on the hourly route 9 service from Colne to Keighley. SRG23 was to remain the only dual door bus in the fleet right up to its eventual withdrawal. However, five REs came in 1966/1967 (SRG34 to 38) with dual door B48D bodies. These were eventually rebuilt to B53F. SRG23 had been an Earls Court Motor 1966 Commercial Motor Show exhibit. Its dual entrance body was the only one in the 1964/1965/1966 intake of SRG 1 to 33 that was not B54F.

Bus Operators

In 1967 there were four companies operating from Waller Hill Bus Station, situated just out of the town centre on the road to Keighley and Bradford: BET's Ribble had a small depot in the town on the A59 Broughton Road with an allocation of around nine vehicles. Tilling's West Yorkshire also had a small shed, and an allocation of around five single deckers, three double deckers and in the summer, a coach. Their Skipton depot was located on the A65, just off Newmarket Street/Otley Road, and was a subsidiary outstation of Keighley, as also was the nearby Grassington depot with three or four single decker buses. Pennine Motor Services' main depot was at Gargrave, 4.2 miles away on the A65 towards Kendal. Pennine also had a very small depot in Skipton, on Jerry Croft at the side of the town hall, along with further small outstations in Settle (for two buses) and Ingleton, shared with Ribble (space for four buses). Ezra Laycock ran in from Barnoldswick and is said to have out-stationed one bus overnight behind a pub in nearby Carleton, the main depot being in West Close Road, Barnoldswick, some 9.1 miles away.

Stage Routes

On the Sunday we visited, the following stage routes were operating:

Operator	Number	Route from Skipton	Sunday journeys	Journey time (one way)
West Yorkshire	10	Keighley via Kildwick	10 journeys	30 minutes
	11	Keighley via Cononley	11 journeys	36 minutes
	67	Keighley and Bradford	13 journeys	68 minutes
	71	Grassington and Buckden	Four full journeys and eight shorts to Grassington	64 minutes
	73	Shortbank Road	Five journeys	7 minutes
	74	Greatwood Avenue and Horse Close Estate	Five journeys	5 minutes
	76	Otley, Harrogate and Tadcaster	Six full journeys, 2 shorts to Harrogate and one to Ikley	2 hours 22 minutes
Ribble	X27	Clitheroe, Preston, Southport and Liverpool	10 journeys and one Clitheroe short	3 hours 52 minutes

Operator	Number	Route from Skipton	Sunday journeys	Journey time (one way)
Ribble	281 and X43	Earby, Colne (281) and Manchester (X43)	12 full journeys and two shorts	2 hours 20 / 2 hours 33 minutes
	S1	Ribble Garage, Broughton Road	27 journeys including the passing by of the X27/X43/281	5 minutes
	S3	Easby and Bolton Abbey	Two journeys	26 minutes
	S6	Embsay and Easby	Three to Easby and 11 short journeys to Embsay	8 minutes to Embsay and 12 minutes to Easby
Laycock		Barnoldswick	Seven journeys	34 minutes
		Carleton +	Eight journeys	10 minutes
		Bradley +	No Sunday service	10 minutes
Pennine	(210)	Gargrave and Malham	Four journeys and one Gargrave short	43 minutes (and joint with Ribble)
	(580) (38 to 40)	Settle, Ingleton, to Lancaster	Lancaster only with three journeys & five (with a change at Ingleton) and four Settle shorts	2 hours 59 minutes (and joint with Ribble)

+ Laycocks had taken over the Carleton and Bradley routes from JY Hey t/a Silver Star of Carleton in August 1961. The Bradley route was not actively pursued by Laycock and was taken up in 1964 by West Yorkshire, who diverted some journeys on its not Sunday Keighley local route 8 to call at Bradley, whilst en route between Skipton and Silsden.

So that was it for stage bus routes on a Sunday. Quite busy really, with the routes for the rest of week having more journeys and some additional routes:

8	To Silsden via:	Six journeys Monday to Friday, plus two shorts to Bradley	30 to 35 minutes
8A	Bradley & Cononley	and one to Crosshills on school days, with on Saturday	
8B	Cononley	four full and four shorts to Bradley.	
8M	Bradley Main Road		
71A	To Litton via Grassington	One journey on a Saturday plus one from Grassington that returned to Skipton.	65 minutes

Silver Star Bedford OB JWW933 with unusual Mulliner body in Skipton BS with Pennine NWT329.

Seasonal Routes

In the summer there were two extended service routes of West Yorkshire that ran via Grassington/ Buckden in Wharefdale, then over into Wensleydale, in Tilling's United Automobile Service (UAS) territory. Route 70 (that earlier had been the 78) operated on a Tuesday, Saturday and Sunday and ran from Leeds/Bradford via Keighley, Skipton, Grassington and Buckden into Wensleydale. Here it turned left for Hawes, a journey time from Skipton of 2 hours 2 minutes. On Saturday and Sunday, the 70 was extended further north, over Buttertubs Pass to Muker, another 35 minute journey.

The other route was on Friday only and started in Skipton. Route 70A (earlier it was the 79) went also to Wensleydale, but then turned right to Leyburn where it finished its 2 hour journey.

West Yorkshire's SGL8 is climbing up Kidstones Pass out of Wensleydale and then will have the drop on the other side into Buckden in Wharefdale. It is headed for Skipton on the Friday run from Leyburn in the early 1960s (by 1966 route 79 had been renumbered to route 70A).

On the seasonal routes, there were many summer express coach services operated by West Yorkshire Road Car and Ribble that either started in Skipton or passed through. These coach services were as follows:

- Leeds/Bradford to Blackpool (Joint WY/Ribble service J5 from Leeds via Pudsey and Shipley, J6 a feeder from Bradford to Skipton with some runs throughs and the J9 from Leeds via Otley)
- Harrogate to Blackpool, (Joint service with W. Pyne of Harrogate, J16)
- Leeds/Bradford to Keswick (Joint WY/Ribble service X87)
- Leeds/Bradford to Morecambe (Joint WY/Ribble service X88)
- Filey, Scarborough to Blackpool (Joint WY/Ribble service X15)
- Skipton to Blackpool (Ribble X16)
- Skipton to Scarborough (WY X76)
- Skipton to Bridlington and Filey (WY X77)
- Skipton to Llandudno and North Wales (Ribble X35)
- Skipton to Southport (Ribble X5)

At peak holiday times these express routes often had duplicates, commonly provided by independents hired in for the day. Blackpool was a magnet, especially with its Illuminations, a clever seasonal extension from the end of August to the first week in November. Blackpool was a true honeypot for buses, especially on a Saturday.

In the late 1950s centre stage for Blackpool is West Yorkshires EG1 a 1949 L5G with ECW DP31R body that, after being delivered in a cream and red livery, was painted red and cream in 1954. In 1959 it became a normal stage bus as SG151 and two years later was sold to Hedingham & District. Alongside is 1956 LD6B DX44 on a 2hour 22 minute run to Tadcaster; this route was formed in 1957 by joining the Skipton to Harrogate route with the Harrogate to Tadcaster route. A LL5G is tucked in behind. In the background on the left is a Silver Star Bedford OB, one of three, two with bus bodies and this one, SMY916. with a Duple Vista body. They ran a short route to Carleton and were taken over by Ezra Laycocks from Barnoldswick in 1961. The cream coloured bus is not identified but is probably a hired duplicate for Blackpool passing through.

West Yorkshire's 1966 RELH ERG8 (renumbered 1008 in 1971) passes through Skipton for Morecambe on an X88. A Pennine Duple Donington and a West Yorkshire MW6G (coded SMG) are in the background.

Buses Operated

West Yorkshire had the most departures on a Sunday followed by Ribble, Laycock and Pennine. So, what buses did we see?

In the bus station was West Yorkshire 1963 Bristol MW SMG26 834BWY on the 71 to Buckden via Grassington. On a Sunday this service ran to Buckden (64 minutes away) with four journeys, whereas Grassington had an additional eight journeys taking 30 minutes. Three SMGs were the usual allocation at Grassington Depot and later in the decade, three Bristol LHs took over, assisted by two SULs from Skipton. The Wharefdale bus routes numbered from 69 to 79 will feature in a future book.

SMG31 on a Skipton local route. The round disc next to the fleet number was for depot coding that started in 1958 but was then abandoned in 1964. This grey-coloured disc was for Keighley and the outstations at Skipton, Ilkley and Grassington.

West Yorkshire Bristol LS SMG41 OWX153 (in the 1955 batch originally numbered EUG26 to 45) was operating on the local route 73 to Short Bank Road. This had five trips on a Sunday, taking just 7 minutes. On its return it then prepared itself for a 71 to Grassington. These Bristol LS buses went through a series of changes during their time with West Yorkshire from being first classified as dual purpose (EUG), then to service buses (SUG) and finally, being re-seated to their maximum capacity, and/or fitted for one man operation (SMG). The batch SUG 26 to 45 were originally EUG25 to 45 and were renumbered in March 1959 when they also retained the dual-purpose seating. However, five years later between March and June 1964, SUG39 to 45 were re-seated to B45F (39/40 by ECW, 41 to 45 by West Yorkshire) and were then renumbered to SMG 39 to 45.

The former EUG41 as SUG 41 after it was downgraded to bus status in March 1959, but still has dual-purpose seating and livery. It is in Skipton Bus Station having worked on a 67, probably only from Keighley and has yet to be reseated and numbered SMG41, which would happen in 1964.

I did not record any other West Yorkshire buses. However, the following are examples of the type of buses used on the Skipton routes. The single deck buses used on the West Yorkshire 11, 71, 73 and 74 routes were as follows:

- SG class, Bristol L5G from 1939 to the mid-50s and fitted with bible indicators.
- SGL Bristol LL5G from the early 1950s to 1965. These were the 1950s workhorses, especially SGL8 to 10 at Grassington.
- EUG/SUG/SMG Bristol LS5G from 1957 to 1970 replaced the SGLs and became the 1960s workhorses, especially SUG2 to 5.
- SMG Bristol MW6G from 1963 to 1974, especially SMG30 to 32 at Grassington.

On the seasonal routes to Hawes and Leyburn in Wensleydale, the following were commonly used:

- EB/SB Bristol L6B from the early 1950s to 1961.
- SBW Bristol LWL6B from the early 1950s to the mid-1960s.
- Later the Bristol LS and MWs were used.

The West Yorkshire double deckers on the 10, 67 and 76 routes were:

- DB Bristol K6B from 1948 to the mid-1960s, (however, Keighley's KDB55 to 57 carried on until 1969).
- DB Bristol KS6B from 1950 to the mid-1960s.
- DBW/DGW Bristol KSW6B/KSW6G from 1951 to 1969.
- DX Bristol LD6B & FS6B from 1954 and 1959 respectively to the late 1970s.

KDB31 on a 10 to Keighley with a Ribble PD3/Burlingham in the background. New in 1949, it was withdrawn in 1966. A DX waits behind on the 76 and across is a Ribble PD3 Burlingham on the X43 for Manchester.

In the bus station was Ribble 673 DRN673D, a 1966 Leyland PSU4/4R with Marshall BET style B45F body and working the S6, a short 8 minute run to Embsay that is the home of the Embsay to Bolton Abbey preserved railway.

673 on a local service parked up in Skipton Bus Station, here with the pre-1969 style of fleet name. Ten of these buses in the CRN/DRNxxxD batch were sold to the Isle of Man in late 1979/early 1980 where they operated up to 1985.

Before these buses, Ribble had regularly used, on their "S" routes, the all Leyland single deckers and double deckers at Skipton.

A picture taken earlier in July 1961 shows a 1960 Atlantean 1685 from Burnley Depot on the X43, Skipton having at the time 1689/90 in their allocation of nine buses. In the background is all Leyland Royal Tiger 392, one of a pair at Skipton. The all Leyland PD2 1306 was also from Skipton Depot and is parked up next to a Pennine 1947 Leyland PS1 with Burlingham B35F body. It is GWT317, due for withdrawal in a month, its sister GWT318 having already gone in January 1960.

We also saw Ribble White Ladies 1270 and 1272 NRN 419/421, 1962 Leyland PDR1/1 Weymann HC50Ft. These rather special buses were on the once per hour Manchester X43 route that required up to ten vehicles with four coming from nearby Burnley and two from Skipton. Ribble had 35 Atlantean White Ladies delivered in two batches; 1251 to 1265 in 1959/1960 and 1266 to 1285 in 1962. By 1973 many were repainted in the normal red bus livery and were used into the late 1970s.

White Lady 1272 with the original Ribble style logo at Manchester Lower Mosely Street Bus Station. 1276 and 1278, were based at Skipton for around 15 years and worked three round trips to Manchester each day with around 20 minutes scheduled break per trip.

Red aka "Scarlet Lady" 1278 in Skipton Bus Station in the NBC era. In the background is a West Yorkshire Plaxton RE from the 1974 batch of five registered NYGxxxM on the 287 (formerly the X87) summer only service from Keswick to Leeds.

The White Ladies were named after the first 30 White Ladies 1201 to 1230 Leyland PD1/3 with Burlingham FCL49RD bodies from 1948 with five bay bodies. These were followed in 1950/1951 by 1231 to 1250, Leyland PD2/3 with East Lancs bodies to the same overall design but with four bays. These were all withdrawn in the early 1960s and latterly worked bus routes, indeed some had been repainted in bus livery in the late 1950s.

Ribble 1247 is one of the Leyland PD2/3 second batch of White Ladies. The name comes from the legendary White Lady ghost, Dorothy Southworth, from Samlesbury Hall near Preston and had originated when the Leyland PD1 first batch was launched at Samlesbury Hall. It was a foggy day, and it was said they looked like ghosts when they appeared out of the mist.

One of the first batch of White Ladies from 1948 with Burlingham body and now in bus livery is Leyland PD1, 1202 BRN262.

In the bus station bound for Southport was Ribble 812 ARN812C, a 1965 Leyland PSU3/3R Weymann DP49F on the X27 to Liverpool via Clitheroe, Preston and Southport; quite a route and taking just under four hours. Ribble 812 (seen here working an X43) demonstrates how a good livery can totally change the appearance for the better, of the standard BET designed body.

The X27 was worked from Liverpool, Southport and Clitheroe depots with Skipton only having limited scheduled operations. Wish I had seen Ribble 955 from 1954 on the X27 from the first batch of Leyland Tiger Cubs. It has a Burlingham Seagull III body with centre entrance; the next batch were Seagull IV's with front entrances.

Ribble 1045, a Leyland Leopard with Harrington Cavalier C41F body from 1961, would be the coach allocated to Skipton. It is here working the former S6 now the 230 after the early 1970s renumbering. Behind on the X43 is low height Atlantean 1668 from 1960.

Now over to an important small operator, Ezra Laycock. They were said to have had the first bus in Yorkshire in 1905 and were eventually to be taken over by Pennine Motor Services in 1972. Originally based at Cowling on the border between Lancashire and Yorkshire, Laycocks moved to Barnoldswick in 1932.

In August 1961 Laycocks purchased J. T. Hey, trading as Silver Star Motor Services. Silver Star had a Skipton to Carleton stage service and a workers' special between Carleton to a mill called Rycroft & Hartley in Broughton Road, Skipton. Silver Star also had operated a Skipton-Bradley route but Laycocks allowed this to lapse.

Silver Star latterly had three Bedford OB's which were operated by Laycocks for two weeks before they were sold::

- JWW933 was new in 1950 with unusual Mulliner bus body.
- SMY916 new April 1948 to a CG Lewis, London with a Duple Vista body and came to Silver Star in the early 1950s.
- GOU721 with a Perkins diesel engine with Duple bus body and was new in 1949 to Kilner, Horsham. It came from Hants and Sussex MS in 1955 when that company was liquidated.

Silver Star GOU721 with Duple bus body crosses the railway bridge in Skipton, bound for Carleton with a full load. The livery was red, grey and cream.

It was initially planned for the Carleton route to fit into the waiting time of buses at Skipton on the Barnoldswick service. The route was eventually however, incorporated into the main Skipton to Barnoldswick route, but Laycock did have a vehicle spend the night in Carleton behind a public house.

Replacements for the ex-Silver Star buses were quickly bought by Laycocks. These arrived as fleet number 60, a Leyland TS from Ribble, and as seen above, 61 in Skipton Bus Station for Carleton, a Tilling-Steven with Duple B39F body that was new in August 1962 to Morrison of Tenby Laycock, Barnoldswick TSM 61 ODE777 with Duple body B39F new in August 1952 to Morrison of Tenby, in Skipton Bus Station for Carleton. It was bought in August 1961 to replace one of the three JT Hey buses but did not last long as it was sold on in March 1962 to Hillcrest of Settle. In the background is a West Yorkshire coach class CUG, a Bristol/ECW LS and to the right what looks like Laycock's Reliance 53.

The first Laycock's bus we saw in 1967 at Skipton was working the Carleton route. It was number 52 DHG 654 from 1956 and was a not too popular integral AEC Monocoach with Park Royal B44F body. In 1954 Laycocks took delivery of 51, their first AEC Monocoach. Unlike most buses that have a separate chassis and body built by different manufacturers, these were built by Park Royal using AEC mechanical equipment and like cars, were built as one integral unit. The Monocoach did not sell well outside Scotland, where the state-owned Bus Group bought most of them.

52 from 1956 was withdrawn in November 1969 and was like sister 51 CHG748 from 1955. 51 had a shorter life and was sold in April 1961 to help finance the two new Duple Britannia coaches 62/63, 5496/5497YG.

Also seen was Laycock 58 347BUP, a 1959 AEC 2MU3RA with early Plaxton Panorama C41F body, bought from Gardiner Spennymoor in December 1960. It was stood in the bus station and was not showing any route.

58 347BUP was withdrawn after 10 years in December 1970. The Plaxton body with its long windows originated in 1958. After that the Panorama body went through many refinements. The design was eventually copied by other bodybuilders, principally when, at the 1972 Commercial Motor Show, Duple introduced a new range of bodies called the Dominant.

Also waiting in the bus station was Laycock 77, 716AVA another AEC Reliance 2MU3RA with Duple Britannia C41F body from April 1961 and bought from Hutchinson, Overtown in December 1966. This one had Carleton on its blind and had only a few more months left, as in December 1967 it was burnt out. 77 was replaced by an AEC Reliance bus numbered 78 with Plaxton Highway DP43F body and is shown later.

Similar coaches to 77 were 62/63 5496/7YG that were bought new in November 1961. 62 here waits in Skipton, with 53 in the background. They were both withdrawn in December 1970.

The range of Laycock's fleet can be seen in the following buses that we did not see on 15th October 1967.

53 WYG540 was an AEC Reliance MU3RV new in from 1959 with a Roe B45F body and worked until 1971, when it was replaced by an ex West Yorkshire LS.

Laycock 66 RKU221, a 1959 late model of an AEC Regal 6821A with Plaxton FDP39F body, was bought in August 1962 from Rhind in Wakefield. It was the regular Carleton bus for many years up to its withdrawal in May 1970 when it was replaced by 84, a Bristol LS from West Yorkshire. The size of side legal lettering also doubles up for the fleet name. A Pennine Duple Donington loads in the background.

69 UHO3 was bought in 1964 and was new to Creamline in Borden in 1959. It was an AEC Reliance 2MU2RA with Harrington C41F body and was to be replaced in 1972 by a new Bedford YRQ with Plaxton Panorama body.

74 along with 75/76 and registered BCK 437, 428,452 were 1947 Leyland PDL1As bought from Ribble in August 1966. These 1947 buses were rebuilt and then rebodied by Burlingham with L53RD bodies in 1955. They were used by Laycock on contract work for Rolls Royce, and for schools. The latter ran mainly from Barnoldswick into Skipton in the morning, after which the buses could often be found parked up in the bus station during the day before returning to Barnoldswick in the afternoon. They had a chequered career with Laycock. 75 hit a low bridge in October 1969 near to Colne and the engine of 76 engine blew up in 1971; only 74 was around when Pennine bought Laycock.

Laycock's fleet in October 1967 therefore was comprised of single deckers 52, 53. 58. 62/63, 66, 69 and 77 along with the double deckers 74 to 76 from Ribble. Double deckers had entered the fleet in 1965 principally for school contracts when the railway from Skipton to Colne closed. The first two double deckers came from Western SMT and lasted only a year, being unsuitable with their open rear entrances and were replaced by 74 to 76 that had rear doors.

For a small fleet, Laycock always had a lot of interest for the enthusiast and between 1967 and the Pennine takeover day in 1972, the following buses joined the fleet:

- 79 PCJ533, an AEC Reliance with Duple coach body, stayed for a year from May 1968.
- 80 ECK927 came from Ribble in August 1968 and was an all Leyland double decker. It was in the fleet when Pennine took over.
- 81 CMJ504D, new to Super, Upminster, was a Ford R192 with Plaxton coach body and stayed from April 1969 until January 1972.
- 82 YDK589 stayed for a year from November 1969 and was another AEC Reliance but with a Harrington Cavalier coach body from Yelloway of Rochdale.
- 83 968CWL was an AEC Regent V from City of Oxford Motor Services with Weymann body and came in February 1970. It was also in the fleet when Pennine took over.
- 84 to 86 and 89, 94/95 were Bristol LS5Gs and are mentioned below.
- 87/88 AUP402/403F, new to Gardiner, Spennymoor and were Bedford VAL70s with Duple coach bodies that came in January 1971 and went in April and January 1972 respectively.
- 90 to 92 MYG759 to 761K were new in January 1972 and were Bedford YRQs with Plaxton Express bodies.
- 93 OWY197K was new in April 1972 and was a Leyland PSU3B/4R with Plaxton Express bodies.

Of these, only 90 to 93 were to enter full service with Pennine.

Laycock 78 in Skipton BS was originally with Creamline in Borden and came in December 1967 from Super Upminster to replace the burnt-out 77. It stayed for four years and gained "new" bus seats out of 75 BCK428 a Leyland PD1A with Burlingham L53RD body ex-Ribble in August 1966, so, 78 then became B45F instead of being DP43F.

In May 1970 84 OWX144 from West Yorkshire replaced AEC Regal 66 on the Carleton route. It was the first of six Bristol LS that were bought in 1970/1971; two more came in from West Yorkshire and three from Bristol OC. The six replaced 53, 58, 62, 63, 66 and 78. These six Bristols were there in August 1972 when Ezra Laycock sold out to Pennine, but none were taken into the Pennine fleet.

Laycocks had expected to make future purchases of more Bristol single deckers and also 70 seat double deckers, but with the Pennine takeover these plans were never to materialise. The final day, the 11th August 1972 was a Friday when a large crowd gathered for the last bus and the vehicle used was the newest, Leyland Leopard number 93. This was, along with Bedfords 90 to 92, taken into the Pennine fleet, and whilst 93 had a full life, the lightweight Bedfords went in 1975.

Laycocks last bus 93 OWY197K went to Pennine where it is seen here in April 1975 leaving Barnoldswick going past the Rolls Royce factory, which is just out of sight to the right on the picture. It was withdrawn around 1992 but kept back for preservation and was initially kept at Ingleton Depot before returning to Barnoldswick.

Perhaps one of the best remembered fleets in the area is Pennine Motor Services (PMS) with their unusual orange, grey and black livery with script fleet name. Skipton Bus Station with Pennine NWT807 for Malham and 240CWY behind for Ingleton and beyond. Then we have a Ribble probably on a local and behind it a White Lady for Manchester on the X43.

In Skipton Bus Station in October 1967 was Pennine LWY702 new in 1953. This was loading for Malham and was an all Leyland PSU1/17 with B44F body and is seen here parked up near the depot in Skipton. LWY702 looks very similar to Ribble's ECK/ERN registered all Leyland's, apart from the non-recessed driver's windscreen and grill which was added later. It was joined in January 1964, by ECK610 from Ribble. LWY702 from 1953 had less than three years' service left and was scrapped in February 1970 and replaced by CWT474H, a new Leyland/Willowbrook in the BET style.

Pennine's ex-Ribble 347, ECK610, was new in 1952 and came in January 1964 as a replacement for JWT724. ECK610 stayed until 1977 to be replaced by UWR712R, a new Leyland/Plaxton.

JWT724 was the last of three similar Leyland PS buses with Burlingham bodies, and very similar to Ribble's 201 to 247. New in May 1950 it had been converted to one man operation but after failing a Ministry examination in December 1963 it was withdrawn and quickly replaced by ex-Ribble ECK610. The engine though was salvaged, machined locally and converted to horizontal for use in a Royal Tiger.

Also in Skipton Bus Station on 15th October was Pennine 240CWY a 1963 Leyland L2 with well-proportioned Roe B47F body. It was bound for Ingleton, a one hour 25-minute journey on the A65.

LWU499D seen here loading for Ingleton was a cousin to 240CWY from May 1963. It came in June 1966 as a Leyland PSU4/3 with three and two seating at the rear giving 49 seats in all, eight more than 240CWY. Both were replaced by Leyland/Plaxtons in 1975 and 1978 and both were to see further service after withdrawal with Tillingbourne Valley in Guildford.

An hour later we saw Pennine UWX 277. This would follow 240CWY up the A65 to Settle and Ingleton from where it would carry on for another 67 minutes to Lancaster. UWX277 was new in 1958 and was a Leyland PSUC1/1 with Duple Donington DP41F body and at one time could have carried on to Morecambe, a 20 minutes trip from Lancaster. As with the Malham route, this route was joint with Ribble, but I never saw Ribble operating these routes. Apparently pre-war on Sundays, Ribble had at least two round trips a day from Lancaster to Skipton. The Morecambe route had become a joint operation in 1931 with a pooled miles and money arrangement; from 1936 the Malham route also had a similar pooled miles/money arrangement. On the Morecambe route, Pennine ran mainly between Skipton and Ingleton, with Ribble doing the leg onto Lancaster and Morecambe, though Pennine did at one time have up to five trips a day to Morecambe.

UWX277 was the first of four similar bodied buses that entered service in 1958, 1960 (6108WU), 1961 (9712WX) and in 1962 (5895YG), the latter two being five bay (Donington 2) with deeper windows and a "cleaner" style than the above seven-bay bodies. UWX277 lasted until June 1973 when it went to another Guildford operator, Browns, and was replaced at Pennine in 1973 by a Plaxton Elite Express Leyland.

At Settle Pennine would meet the bus from Hillcrest that ran up to Horton in Ribblesdale. In 1966 they bought LTB787, a 1949 Leyland Comet with Bellhouse Hartwell C33F body that had been new to Ireland of Lancaster. The destination "papers" may be seen in the roof front windows as it waits in Settle for its next journey. LTB787 had replaced a Tilling-Stevens, which in turn had replaced a similar one registered ODE777 that had been with Laycock until 1962 and had lasted three years with Hillcrest before an engine failure in 1965. Hillcrest had started in 1956 as an amalgamation of three operators and later in that year, another one joined. At the time they operated mainly school contracts and carried on with this work until acquiring Anderson of Settle in 1962 who had the 8 mile route from Settle to Horton in Ribblesdale. In 1968 the Comet became a back-up to a Bedford/Willowbrook bus bought from The Eden of West Auckland. Hillcrest lasted until 1974 and the route then passed through a succession of operators.

Being a Sunday, we only saw three of the Pennine fleet, which in October 1967 also included the following buses. All were bought new, except the first two and ECK610:

- MTC757 Leyland PSU1/13 Brush B43F in November 1951 ex-Leyland demonstrator
- MTD235 Leyland PSU1/15 Leyland C41C in September 1952 ex-Leyland demonstrator with the prototype coach body
- NWT329 Leyland PSU1/14 with Roe B44F body in May 1954
- NWT807 Leyland PSU1/14 with Roe DP44F body in June 1954
- 6108WU Leyland PSUC1/2 with Duple Donington DP41F body in April 1960
- 9712WX Leyland PSUC1/2 with Duple Donington DP41F body in May 1961
- 5895YG Leyland L2 with Duple Donington DP41F body in January 1962
- ECK610 Leyland PSU1/13 with Leyland B44F body in January 1964 ex-Ribble
- FWX554C Leyland PSU3/3R with Plaxton C49F body in May 1965
- LWU499D Leyland PSU4/4R with Roe B49F body in June 1966, and soon to come was:
- UWU521F Leyland PSU4/4R with Willowbrook DP41F body in April 1968

What were no longer in the fleet in 1967 were some splendid Leyland PS Tigers with Burlingham bodies that were "clones" of those with Ribble. Some of these vehicles are illustrated on the following pages.

Ribble "clones" GWT317 like GWT318 were Leyland PS1, new in 1947 with Burlingham B35F bodies and worked on until 1961 and 1960 respectively when they seem to have been replaced by Donington's 9712WX and 6108WU.

In Skipton Bus Station Leyland PS1 HYG60 from 1949 with rarish Wallace Arnold owned Wilks & Meade body. It was originally in the coach cream and orange livery and was replaced in 1962 by Duple Donington 5895YG.

In the cream and orange coach livery is HYG309 a Leyland PS2 with Burlingham body from 1949. It lasted three years more than HYG60 and was later painted in the orange bus livery. Plaxton Panorama bodied FWX554C replaced it in 1965.

Back to the fleet in 1967 and we will start with the former Leyland demonstrators. 1967 was also the year one person operation (OPO) was introduced and by 1970 all operations were OPO, with staffing reduced from thirty three to twenty three.

Leyland demonstrator MTC757 from 1951 and a Commercial Vehicle Show exhibit was an early underfloor engined bus and waits in Skipton. MTC was taken out of service in August 1967 and scrapped; UWU521F replaced it but that was soon sold in 1970 as it had a small number of seats, as from 1969, Leyland/Willowbrook DP49F bodies were bought. UWU had been bought as it was thought that 36foot buses would be unsuitable.

MTD235 from 1950 was a Leyland demonstrator of the new coach bodywork that was bought by many BET fleets and appeared at the Commercial Vehicle Show. I is seen here on hire to Ribble or West Yorkshire on the Lisbon Street spare land near to Wellington Street Bus Station that was used on summer Saturdays. It came to Pennine in 1952 and was replaced in 1970 by CWT101H, the second Leyland/ Willowbrook DP49F. Stored from 1970 for over 30 years by Pennine and then by the owner's Simpson family, it is currently undergoing restoration and will make a great historical contribution to the preservation movement.

In the sun at Malham is NWT329. It and NWT807 came in 1954 and both served for 20 years and were replaced by Leyland/Plaxtons. Their Roe bodies looked as normal for Roe, "fit for purpose".

9712WX with the cleaner looking five-bay Duple Donington 2 body. New in 1961 when it replaced PS1 GWT317, it is waiting in Skipton. 9712WX went in 1972 to Tillingbourne Valley in Guildford and was replaced at Pennine by OWR265K a Leyland/Plaxton Elite Express.

Resting off stand at Lancaster Bus Station, with the driver reading his newspaper on the 40 minute layover. In the early 1950s this was a 3 hour 10 minutes journey from Skipton but reduced in the 1960s to 2 hours 24 minutes. FWX554C from 1965 was the first of many Plaxtons bought by Pennine and was in the cream and orange coach livery when new. It had replaced Leyland PS HYG309 in 1965 but only stayed until 1971 when it was replaced by a Leyland/Willowbrook HWU816J. I suspect its manual front door could have been a problem on stage work, as Pennine was all OPO by 1970.

CWT474H had replaced all Leyland LWY702 and is loading at Malham, for a 43 minute journey to Skipton. Between 1968 and 1971 three other similar Leylands with Willowbrook DP49F BET styled bodies were bought (CWU101H and HWU 816/817J), these three replacing MTD235, FWX55C and UWU521F. Thereafter from 1972 to 1990 Leyland/Plaxton Elites, many the Express version, were the bus of choice.

OWR265/266K were the first Leylands with Plaxton Elite bodies and came in April and June 1972 respectively. 266 is here at Skipton and had replaced Donington 9712WX which went to Tillingbourne Valley in Guildford.

JWU798N was one of the many Pennine Leyland/Plaxton Elite Express C49F. From 1973 to 1975 six were bought (UWX596L, RWY378 to 379M and JWU797 to 799N), and replaced 6108WU, 240CWY, 5895YG, NWT329 and 807, along with the three 1972 acquired Laycock Bedford YRQs that were withdrawn in 1975.

So that is my view of the marvellous Pennine fleet that shows the buses and routes they had in 1967, along with some of the earlier buses, plus, a brief look at the 1967 fleet and, what replaced them. After 1972, Leyland/Plaxtons were the main choice and the last new one came in 1980; thereafter, the purchases of Leyland/Plaxtons were all second-hand, apart from two new 1991 Leyland Swifts that were quickly sold after nine months. Concentration after these Swifts was now on "pure" buses, first with Leyland Nationals and by 1999 eighteen Nationals had been with Pennine. These were replaced by sixteen second-hand Dennis Darts in the 2000s, a time when the bus industry continued to change, with the gradual reduction of subsidies to operators and reductions in the rebate paid for concessionary travel. This was to cause a "slow death" cumulative effect for Pennine and very sadly Pennine ceased operations on 16th May 2014.

A final surprise in 1967

We were not yet finished as it was a short walk to the West Yorkshire depot and there, to my surprise in the field behind the depot, was parked up Ledgards CRN852 and 866. Now Ledgards had only been taken over by West Yorkshire on the previous day, so it seemed that buses were being dispersed from the Ledgard depots to await their final disposal. CRN852 and 866 were from the Ledgard Moorfield Depot at Yeadon where they had operated on the two Otley to Horsforth routes.

The wholesale removal of Ledgards fleet away from the former Ledgard depots is another story, but suffice to note here, that the following were to join CRN852/856 at Skipton:

- From Ledgard Armley (Leeds): Ex-RTs LLU803/842/843/873, MLL834 and ex-Felix all Leyland JWU131

- From Ledgard Otley: Ex-Preston all Leylands ARN393/394, BCK621/633 and ex-Bristol OC Leyland/ECW KHY395

Skipton got the lowest number of former Ledgard buses and the remainder of the Ledgard fleet went to the West Yorkshire depots in Harrogate, York and Bradford. West Yorkshire kept twelve double deckers and two coaches and operated them for a short time.

Ledgard all Leyland ex-Ribble CRN852 at Otley waiting to depart on its normal service to Horsforth near Leeds that required lowbridge buses.

Ledgards ex-Preston all Leyland BCK621 at Skipton came from Otley Depot where it operated local town routes and to Leeds and Ilkey.

BCK621 seen just a few months earlier in service at Otley.